First Facts®

Marie Curie

PHYSICIST AND CHEMIST

Lisa M Bolt Simons

Raintree is an imprint of Capstone Global Library Limited, a company incorporated in England and Wales having its registered office at 264 Banbury Road, Oxford, OX2 7DY – Registered company number: 6695582

www.raintree.co.uk
myorders@raintree.co.uk

Edited by Anna Butzer
Designed by Bobbie Nuytten
Picture research by Jo Miller
Production by Laura Manthe
Originated by Capstone Global Library Limited
Printed and bound in India.

ISBN 978 1 4747 5536 8 (hardcover)   ISBN 978 1 4747 5538 2 (paperback)
22 21 20 19 18   23 22 21 20 19 18
10 9 8 7 6 5 4 3 2 1   10 9 8 7 6 5 4 3 2 1

British Library Cataloguing in Publication Data
A full catalogue record for this book is available from the British Library.

Acknowledgements
We would like to thank the following for permission to reproduce photographs: Getty Images: Hulton Archive, cover, Jacques Boyer, 19, Popperfoto, 17; Newscom: Ann Ronan Picture Library Heritage Images, 7, 15, Fine Art Images/Album, 9, Oxford Science Archive Heritage Images, 21; Science Source: American Institute of Physics/Physics Today Collection, 11; Shutterstock: Everett Historical, 5, 13

Design Elements: Shutterstock: matthew25

Contents

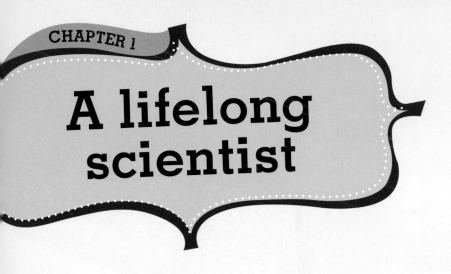

CHAPTER 1

A lifelong scientist

In 1903 Marie Curie won a Nobel Prize in **Physics**. She was the first woman to do so. Eight years later she won the Nobel Prize in **Chemistry**. She's the only person to win this prize in two different sciences. These Nobel Prizes are just two of Marie's honours as a lifelong scientist.

physics study of matter and energy, including light, heat, electricity and motion

chemistry scientific study of substances, what they are composed of and the ways they react with each other

FACT Marie Curie was the first person to win the Nobel Prize twice.

CHAPTER 2

Blooming scientist

Maria "Manya" Sklodowska was born in Warsaw, Poland, on 7 November 1867. Both of her parents were teachers. At the time, Poland was part of the Russian Empire. Maria had four older brothers and sisters. Maria's father taught her some science.

"I am among those who think that science has great beauty."

Marie Curie

Marie (far left) with her father and sisters, 1886

Maria graduated from secondary school when she was 15. Then she moved to Krakow, Poland, which was ruled by Austria. She **tutored** children. When she was 24, Maria moved to Paris, France. She wanted to study maths and physics. She changed her name to Marie, the French spelling of Maria.

Studying in secret

Maria went to a "Floating University" in Warsaw. It changed locations all the time because it was a secret from the Russians. It taught illegal classes such as Polish history.

tutor provide extra help for pupils outside school

Marie, aged 16

CHAPTER 3

Teacher and researcher

A few years after Marie moved to Paris, she met Pierre Curie. He was also a scientist. They married in 1895. Marie became the head of her husband's physics **laboratory** after he got a new job. Marie and Pierre discovered **polonium** and **radium**. They are chemical elements. Marie and Pierre found radium to have healing abilities.

"It would be a beautiful thing to pass through life together hypnotized in our dreams: your dream for your country; our dream for humanity; our dream for science."

Pierre Curie to Marie Sklodowska

Marie and Pierre in the lab

laboratory place where scientists do experiments and tests

polonium silvery-grey element that is very radioactive

radium white radioactive metal element; radium can be harmful when not used correctly

Marie earned her Doctor of Science (PhD) degree in Physics in 1903. She was the first woman in France to get this degree. The same year, she and her husband shared the Nobel Prize in Physics. The Curies also won the Davy Medal for exceptional research in chemistry. Pierre died three years later.

FACT A horse and carriage hit Pierre as he crossed a street on 19 April 1906. He died instantly.

Pierre and Marie Curie, 1903

After Pierre's death, Marie took over her husband's teaching job. It was the first time a woman had taught at that university. She wrote a 971-page paper on **radioactivity** in 1910. The next year Marie won her second Nobel Prize. The prize for chemistry honoured her discovery of polonium and radium.

radioactivity process in which atoms break apart and create a lot of energy

Marie in her laboratory, 1920

FACT In 1910 Marie could not join the French Academy of Sciences because she was a woman.

During World War I (1914–1918), Marie set up X-ray machines to help doctors who performed surgeries. Marie even put X-ray machines in ambulances and drove them to the front lines. Marie and her oldest daughter, Irène, also encouraged the use of radium to help soldiers in pain.

Gifted girls

While the Curies' older daughter joined them in science, their younger daughter, Ève, became a journalist. She wrote a book about Marie in 1937.

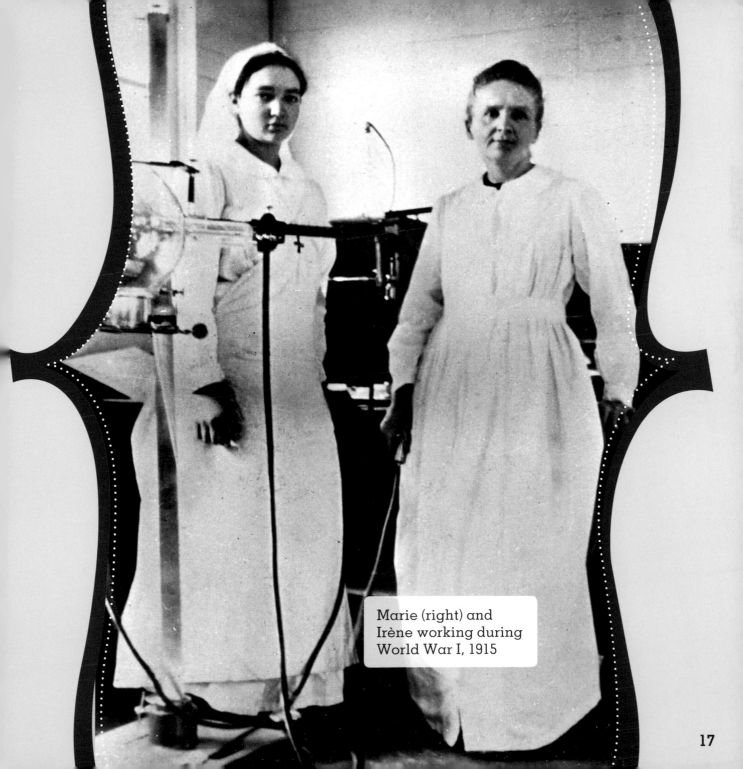

Marie (right) and Irène working during World War I, 1915

CHAPTER 4

Worldwide respect

Marie was recognized for her work around the world. Universities, such as the University of Birmingham in the UK, gave her **honorary** degrees. Clubs and societies gave her honorary memberships. She published her work in science magazines. She also wrote three books on her findings.

honorary given as a gift or in appreciation without the usual requirements

A friendly donation

In 1929 US President Hoover awarded Marie $50,000. The American Friends of Science donated the money. Marie used it to buy radium for her lab in Poland.

Marie speaking at the Conservatory of Arts and Crafts in Paris, France, 1925

On 4 July 1934, Marie died at the age of 66 of aplastic anaemia. She had worked with **radiation** most of her life. It caused the disease that killed her. In 1935 Irène Curie and her husband received the Nobel Prize in Chemistry. Although they won separately, Marie and Irène are the only mother and daughter Nobel Prize winners.

"I am working in the laboratory all day long, it is all I can do: I am better off there than anywhere else."

Marie Curie

radiation rays of energy given off by certain elements

Marie (right) and Irène, 1925

Glossary

chemistry scientific study of substances, what they are composed of and the ways they react with each other

honorary given as a gift or in appreciation without the usual requirements

laboratory place where scientists do experiments and tests

physics study of matter and energy, including light, heat, electricity and motion

polonium silvery-grey element that is very radioactive

radiation rays of energy given off by certain elements

radioactivity process in which atoms break apart and create a lot of energy

radium white radioactive metal element; radium can be harmful when not used correctly

tutor provide extra help for pupils outside school

Find out more

Books

Marie Curie (Great Women in Science), Erin Edison (Capstone Press, 2014)

Marie Curie (Super Scientists), Sarah Ridley (Franklin Watts, 2014)

Science (100 Facts), Chris Oxlade (Miles Kelly, 2014)

Website

www.dkfindout.com/uk/science/famous-scientists/ marie-curie

Learn more about Marie Curie. You can also take a quiz about Marie and other famous scientists.

Comprehension questions

1. Why did Marie attend a "Floating University"? Why were they important at the time?

2. Do you think women still have problems getting into organizations as Marie did? Can you give any examples?

3. Why do you think the author started the book with Marie's Nobel Prizes?

Index